MW01118656

Presented to:

_____

Presented by:

_____

Date:

_____

Thanks
For Being a
DAD

Thanks for Being a Dad

©2004 Elm Hill Books
ISBN: 1-40418-547-X

Manuscript written and compiled by Patricia Lutherbeck in association with Snapdragon Editorial Group, Inc.

Products from Elm Hill Books may be purchased in bulk for educational, business, fundraising, or sales promotional use. For information, please email SpecialMarkets@ThomasNelson.com

Introduction

Thank for Being a Dad was created to honor all dads, but especially the one in your life. Let it serve as a simple and heartfelt "thank you" for all the wisdom, love, and protection your dad has provided through the years.

As you read, we hope you will be moved to outwardly express your love and respect for your dad. Honor him for sticking with you through good times and bad. Tell him what it means to you that he's there—loving and caring and ready to help. And thank God for placing such a wonderful dad in your life.

The Publisher

I'm just as lucky as I can be,

for the world's best Dad belongs to me.

Table of Contents

The greatest gift I ever had

came from God; I call him Dad!

Be kind to thy father,

for when thou wert young,

Who loved thee so fondly as he?

He caught the first accents

that fell from thy tongue,

And joined in thy innocent glee.

A Father's Love

The aim of such instruction
is love that comes from a pure heart,
a good conscience, and sincere faith.

1 Timothy 1:5 NRSV

There is something ultimate

in a father's love,

something that cannot fail,

something to be believed

against the whole world.

*The love of a father
is one of nature's
greatest masterpieces.*

One of the best legacies

a father can leave his children

is to love their mother.

We need good fathers in our homes

whose hearts are full of grace.

Who by their love and earnest prayers,

make home a pleasant place.

When I was a boy of fourteen,

my father was so ignorant

I could hardly stand to have

the old man around.

But when I got to be twenty-one,

I was astonished at how much the

old man had learned in seven years.

A Father's Wisdom

Wisdom is a tree of life
to those who take hold of her;
and happy are all who retain her.

---✳---

Proverbs 3:18 NKJV

One father is more

than a hundred schoolmasters.

The older I get, the smarter
my father seems to get.

In times of trouble

you can count on yourself.

In times of disaster

you can count on your friends.

In times of sorrow

you can count on your Father.

My father's advice
would have made me
a better man if
I had heeded it more often.

I cannot think of any need

in childhood as strong

as the need for

a father's protection.

A Father's Protection

The name of the LORD is a strong tower;
the righteous run to it and are safe.

---- ❄ ----

PROVERBS 18:10 NRSV

Safe, for a child

is his father's hand,

holding him tight.

*A dad is a man who seems
to his children the haven
from all harm.
And who makes them certain
that whatever happens —
it will all come out right.*

When I was a kid,

I used to imagine animals

running under my bed.

I told my dad,

and he solved the problem by

cutting off the legs of the bed.

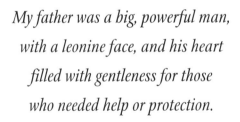

*My father was a big, powerful man,
with a leonine face, and his heart
filled with gentleness for those
who needed help or protection.*

My Pa can sweeten up a day

That clouds and rain make gray.

And tell me funny stories

That will chase the clouds away.

A Father's Nature

*Fathers. . .take your children by the hand
and lead them in the way of the Master.*

————— ✳ —————

EPHESIANS 6:4 MSG

My father didn't
do anything unusual.
He only did what dads are
supposed to do—be there.

Always the same hardworking dad,
plodding day after day;
Thereby ready to meet all the bill
that are ever around to be paid.

My father opened

the jar of pickles

when no one else could.

He was the only one in the house

who wasn't afraid to go

into the basement by himself.

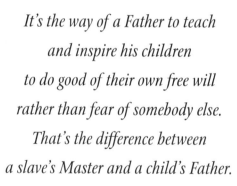

*It's the way of a Father to teach
and inspire his children
to do good of their own free will
rather than fear of somebody else.
That's the difference between
a slave's Master and a child's Father.*

A father is . . .

an ordinary man doing his best

to stand in for Superman. . .

a source of good

but usually expendable advice. . .

a very—nearly expert. . .

a man who knows—

but would like to look it up

just to be on the safe side. . .

a man who goes down fighting.

It's only when you grow up,
and step back from him,
or leave him for your own career
and your own home—
it's only then that you can measure his
greatness and fully appreciate it.
Pride reinforces love.

A father carries pictures

where his money used to be.

*A truly rich man is one
whose children run into his arms
when his hands are empty.*

We do not care how many wrinkles he may have

or how his rheumatism makes him limp

or how the gray colors his hair,

he is still the same great man

and the object of our love and adoration.

*Sometimes the poorest man leaves his
children the richest inheritance.*

What Are Fathers Made Of?

God took the strength of a mountain,

the majesty of a tree,

The warmth of a summer sun,

the calm of a quiet sea,

The generous soul of nature,
the comforting arm of night,
The wisdom of the ages,
the power of the eagle's flight,

The joy of a morning in spring,

the faith of a mustard seed,

The patience of eternity,

the depth of a family need,

Then God combined these qualities;
when there was nothing more to add,
He knew His masterpiece was complete,
And so, He called him . . . Dad.

What Should
We Call Him?

If he's wealthy and prominent,

and you stand in awe of him,

call him "Father."

*If he sits in his shirt sleeves
and suspenders at a ball game
and picnic, call him "Pop."*

If he wheels the baby carriage

and carries bundles meekly,

call him "Papa"

(with the accent on the first syllable).

*If he belongs to a literary circle
and writes cultured papers,
call him "Papa"
(with the accent on the last syllable).*

If, however, he makes a pal of you

when you're good and is too wise

to let you pull the wool over

his loving eyes when you're not;

If, moreover, you're quite sure
no other fellow you know
has quite so fine a father,
you may call him "Dad."

I talk and talk,

and I haven't taught people

in fifty years what my father

taught by example in one week.

MARIO CUOMO

In Praise of Fathers

The glory of children is their father.

———✳———

PROVERBS 17:6 NKJV

What Do I Owe to My Father?

What do I owe to my father? Everything.

He was my best friend:

a parent who knew how to be patient

with an unruly child;

A preacher of joyful faith,
who practiced what he taught;
A good companion in the woods
and the library;
A fearless man with a kind heart;
a Christian without pretense or bigotry;
A true American gentleman
of the democratic type.
Every day I give thanks for him.

———— ❋ ————

HENRY VAN DYKE

*M*y father gave me the greatest gift

anyone could give another person,

he believed in me.

———✳———

JIM VALVANO

My father didn't tell me how to live;
he lived, and let me watch him do it.

CLARENCE B. KELLAND

My best training came from my father.

※

WOODROW WILSON

My dear father; my dear friend;
the best and wisest man I ever knew,
who taught me many lessons
and showed me many things
as we went together
along the country by-ways.

SARAH ORNE JEWETT

I watched a small man

with thick calluses on both hands

work fifteen and sixteen hours a day.

I saw him once literally bleed

from the bottoms of his feet,

a man who came here uneducated,

alone, unable to speak the language,

who taught me all I needed to know

about faith and hard work

by the simple eloquence of his example.

MARIO CUOMO

My dad and I hunted and fished together.

How could I get angry at this man

who took the time to be with me?

DR. JAMES DOBSON

A Letter to Dad

*The other day, I found myself trying
to imagine what it would feel like
to be someone else—someone more
successful, more attractive, more intelligent,
perhaps. I was having a great time
of it when suddenly a terrible thought
occurred to me. If I were someone else,
you wouldn't be my dad.
That would definitely be a problem.
What if the dad of the other person
I would like to be couldn't hit a softball
with one arm behind his back?*

What if he couldn't whistle while he shaved
or make root beer barrels pop out of his ears?
What if that "other" dad wasn't fond
of hugging or telling stupid jokes?
What if he didn't have kind eyes
or a warm smile?
After considering those things,
I realized that I simply couldn't risk becoming
someone else—no matter how
much of a personal upgrade that might be.
You're one in a million
and I'm blessed to call you Dad.

YOUR DAUGHTER,
ANDREA GARNEY

My Dad

As tough as a gorilla,
As big as a bear,
That's my Dad.

As soft as a puppy,
As warm as a furry blanket,
That's my Dad.

As nice as a kitten,
As smart as Albert Einstein,
That's my Dad.

As funny as a clown,
As fast as an athlete,
That's my Dad.

JONATHAN, AGE 9

I love my Dad.
Even when he's tired,
my Daddy has plenty of love
left over for me!

BRENNA, AGE 6

Reference Page

Quote Attribution Page

Margaret Courtney (8), Frederick W. Faber (10), C. Neil Strait (12), Walter Isenhour (13), Mark Twain (14), English Proverb (16), Tim Russett (17), Chae Richardson (18), Philip Greenslade (19), Sigmund Freud (20), Marion C. Garrety (22), Clara Ortega (23), Lou Brock (24), Theodore Roosevelt (25), Marjorie Rawlings (26), Max Lucado (28), Sunday School Banner (29), Erma Bombeck (30), Terrence (31), Pam Brown (32), Margaret Truman (33), Leroy Brownlow (36), Ruth E. Renkel (37),William Franklin (42), Mario Cuomo (48, 56), Henry Van Dyke (50), Jim Valvano (52), Clarence B. Kelland (53), Woodrow Wilson (54), Sarah Orne Jewett (55), Dr. James Dobson (57), Andrea Garney (58), Jonathan Lutherbeck (60), Brenna Hollis (61).